The Gifts of the Spirit

A Judaic Perspective

I0423719

M Debono-De-Laurentis

ISBN: 9781534997691
:

Bible Versions

- Scriptures marked KJV are taken from the KING JAMES VERSION (KJV): KING JAMES VERSION, public domain.
- Scriptures marked CJB are Taken from the Complete Jewish Bible by David H. Stern. Copyright © 1998. All rights reserved. Used by permission of Messianic Jewish Publishers, 6120 Day Long Lane, Clarksville, MD 21029. www.messianicjewish.net.

Dedication

This book is dedicated to all those wonderful Biblically centered and well educated teachers who have helped clarify truth. Dr. Bruce Booker for his keeping me on track and his friendship, and Rabbi Snitkin for his wonderful encouragement. Also to my beautiful wife in putting up with my constant study and computer time, and of course my dear friend Dorothe Kaufmann who so patiently and painstakingly corrected my punctuation and spelling.

Table of Contents

Forward

Dr. Max Debono-De-Laurentis combines his love for the people of God and his desire to teach the Torah correctly from a historical Jewish perspective once again to correct many of the modern approaches to understanding God's Word.

In the following pages you will be confronted with a reality of the great deception the modern-day congregations have come to believe as truth rather than being good Bereans and searching the scriptures to justify what they have been taught as truth. The Bereans would put to the test whatever they were being fed as truth against the total of the Tanakh to determine if it was safe to take in or poison to the soul and spirit. As a result of this approach to the teachings they were considered more noble and mature than many other congregations.

You will find in this brief corrective overview why using an approach of historical Jewish understanding of the times and scriptures brings clarity to the truth of Yeshua's teachings as presented by the apostles. I trust you will be thankful, as I am, for Dr. Max's labor in bringing us back to a first century understanding of what was taught, how it was taught and why it was presented in a Jewish reality and not a Hellenistic pagan perversion.

May the Spirit of God bring us all into the light and truth of correct Torah teachings.

Harry (Rabbi) Robert Snitkin

Introduction

This study will start by examining a Scripture that is often misinterpreted when referring to the Spirit.

> Acts 10:45 and they of the circumcision which believed were astonished, as many as came with Peter, because that on the gentiles also was poured out the gift[1] of the Holy Ghost

It is often wrongly assumed that this event took place at Pentecost/Shavuot, it did not. This event took place much later, but this Scripture does demonstrate that the Holy Spirit is given as a *gift.* The Spirit is not something we earn, nor is it poured out on us as we deserve time after time. This Scripture is clearly pointing to the outpouring of the Spirit upon the gentiles for the first time in Caesarea; this was the first time they were properly witnessed to about Yeshua and were beginning to accept Him as Messiah.

It is important to understand this event took place approximately ten years after Pentecost/Shavuot when the Spirit was first given to the Jewish believers which is totally in line with scripture:

---

[1]**G1431**
δωρεαὶ
dōrea
do-reh-ah'
From G1435; a *gratuity:* - gift.

Acts 1:8 KJV

> But ye shall receive power, after that the Holy Ghost is come upon you: and ye shall be witnesses unto me both in Jerusalem, and in all Judea, and in Samaria, and unto the uttermost part of the earth.

This is the order the Gospel of salvation was to go out into the world – to the Jew first[2], then to the Samaritans who were Jews but considered apostate because they inter married, worshiped at another mountain and refused the ordinances of the rabbis by not following the oral traditions (later to become known as the Oral Law). Finally reaching the nations or gentiles. Please note it was Yeshua Himself who proclaimed this order and as we read through the book of Acts, we see this is exactly how the Gospel was Spread.

However, before anyone can receive the Holy Spirit one must be saved. Today the issue of salvation has lost much of its meaning and has been watered down to what I call a social gospel rather than one of salvation. Let me explain!

Most preachers, evangelists and Christians in general are under the impression that all one need do to be saved is say a prayer to Jesus saying your sorry for your sin and believe in Him. This formula is deemed sufficient and it is usually loudly declared that that person is now saved and

---

[2]Romans 1:16 KJV

> For I am not ashamed of the gospel of Christ: for it is the power of God unto salvation to every one that believeth; to the Jew first, and also to the Greek.

they should have the Holy Spirit to prove it.

In some cases (but by no means all), the first thing that is said is; "you now have the spirit, so prove it by speaking in tongues", a topic we will cover thoroughly in a later chapter.

However, this formula is nowhere found in scripture and does not explain what repentance is. There is also little teaching on the resurrection of the dead, another important but neglected aspect of understanding salvation and what is to come as a result. But even when it does touch upon the subject it tends to be taught that repentance is a turning around from unbelief in Jesus/Yeshua to a belief in Him.

However, this description is not accurate as there is no salvation in this formula but a deception leading to the end time apostate church. Having said that though, there are people who can discover the true meaning of salvation after this event, not because they were saved by the event but because they are true seekers. This makes for an important difference that must be recognized:

> Isaiah 59:1-3 CJB
> Adonai's arm is not too short to save, nor is his ear too dull to hear. Rather, it is your own crimes that separate you from your God; your sins have hidden his face from you, so that he doesn't hear. For your hands are stained with blood and your fingers with crime; your lips speak lies, your tongues utter wicked things.

John 9:31 KJV Now we know that God heareth not sinners: but if any man be a worshipper of God, and doeth his will, him he heareth.

If there is no salvation being given by these prayers because Adonai Himself will not hear the prayers of the unrighteous, what are we left with?

According to John 9:31 we are left with those who worship and obey God, and not those that have just said a prayer. Obedience is a key part of the Gospel message and of major importance when relating to salvation.

In Islam all one need do is declare the five pillars of Islam to irrevocably become a Muslim, and this christian prayer formula is considered to be the same thing. A quick few words to declare your affiliation to a religion but in no way does this make one a christian, any more than being born in a christian family makes one a christian.

So how do we get saved?

Salvation

Salvation is actually dependent upon certain issues despite what today's teachers say: to gain salvation one must first believe, repent and obey.

1. Believe that Yeshua died on a stake/cross and rose again. As a result He took the punishment we deserve for disobeying His Commandments or Torah. Understand that within the teachings of the Torah there are punishments laid out for the trespasser as a result of sin/disobedience. It is these punishments that Yeshua suffered and died to take upon Himself so we don't receive the designated punishment due for our disobedience. He takes it in our stead. He is the FINAL sacrifice once and for all.

2. Repent: - Repentance is turning from your sin to follow God's Commandments – Yeshua said, If you love me obey my commandments. In other words leave your ways and follow the teachings of Torah[3], the righteous lifestyle declared by God

3. Obey God's commandments.

Once these criteria are understood and

---

[3] Torah – known today as the Law but actually means the teachings of God and not legalistic Laws as promoted. Genesis to Deuteronomy.

accepted we can see that first Salvation is granted by God through His grace and once this is done the Holy Spirit is given freely as a gift. We cannot be saved without the Spirit first revealing to us what God has done. We are lead to understand and accept the above points. Once we have accepted what has been made clear in scripture and acknowledge the truth of it, the Spirit will come upon us, in power at the point of Redemption for us to receive the miracle of Salvation.

We can realize the truth of these statements when it is recognized that the Spirit was given to us all, Jew and gentile for a purpose:

> Ezekiel 36:26 KJV I will give you a new heart and put a new spirit inside you; I will take the stony heart out of your flesh and give you a heart of flesh.

It is the next verse that tells us why this is so!

> Ezekiel 36:27 KJV I will put my Spirit inside you and cause you to live by my laws, respect my rulings and obey them.

These verses are accepted as prophetic and pointing to Pentecost/Shavuot. That being the case, how is it missed that the main purpose of the spirit being given is to help us obey and live the Torah lifestyle.

God will put a new Spirit (The Holy Spirit) within us to help us obey His commandments (Law, Torah). That is the purpose of the Comforter, Ruach HaKodesh or Holy Spirit. God sent His Spirit to point us to Him, to live the Holy Lifestyle He requires of us. The Spirit is given by His grace to help us live the life He wants for us. To lead us into all truth.

We are not saved by following the commandments He set out but we are led into sanctification through our obedience to them. We are saved by Grace, so that we cannot say I made it on my own merit and worked my way to God. This is what the cults teach.

No, we are saved from the punishment we deserve for not following His commandments, this is the sins Yeshua died for on the Cross/Stake. Sin is disobeying God's righteous lifestyle and so having need of atonement. Yeshua became that final sacrifice, the final atonement removing the punishment we deserve for disobedience:

> 1 John 3:4 CJB Whosoever committeth sin transgresseth also the law: for sin is the transgression of the law.

Or as the CJB translates so accurately:

> 1 John 3:4 CJB Everyone who keeps sinning is violating Torah—indeed, sin is violation of Torah.

With this in mind, let us continue:

Acts 11:16-17 KJV Then remembered I the word of the Lord, how that he said, John indeed baptized with water; but ye shall be baptized with the Holy Ghost. Forasmuch then as God gave them the like gift as he did unto us, who believed on the Lord Jesus Christ; what was I, that I could withstand God?

- Them = gentiles
- Gift = Gratuity (See Footnote on Page 1)
- Us = Jewish Believers

Scripture reminds us that it was only after the gentiles were brought into salvation, grafted into the Judaic faith of the Messiah that it made sense from a Scriptural point of view to the Jews who came to them. It made sense of Peters vision where gentiles would be grafted into the Judaic faith in the Jewish Messiah.

The idea that the Jewish people no longer have salvation because they killed the Messiah should be put to bed. The event in Ceasaria didn't take place until 10 years after Pentecost. Realizing this can lead one to see that the large numbers of believers initially spoken of being brought into salvation were in fact the Jewish people.

Knowing that the event at Pentecost was for the Jewish believers only and was a fulfilment of both prophecy, and the completing of the integration with man and God's Comforter/Holy Spirit will help us to understand the spiritual gifts:

in the context and correct use meant for us as believers, both then and now.

> Act 2:38 KJV Then Peter said unto them, Repent, and be baptized every one of you in the name of Jesus Christ for the remission of sins, and ye shall receive the <u>gift</u> of the Holy Ghost. *(The Gift of the Spirit, not the gifts of the Spirit. My emphasis)*

When Peter speaking this he was only witnessing to the Jews at this time (gentiles weren't witnessed to yet). After Pentecost, all those who came to the faith gained a completion with the Holy Spirit at conversion. This is them being made complete in their relationship with Adonai. Yeshua Himself gave direction as to how to spread the Gospel: first to Jerusalem then Judea and Samaria and then to the rest of the world. Notice it was all Jews and Samaritans witnessed to first before the gentiles.[4]

The Samaritans were also of the Jewish faith, though they had perverted many of the teachings. They were classed as apostate or backslidden Jews.

I have often heard Acts 3:38 KJV interpreted this way:

When you are saved, you will receive the gifts of the Spirit.

---

[4] Acts 1:8 KJV But ye shall receive power, after that the Holy Ghost is come upon you: and ye shall be witnesses unto me both in Jerusalem, and in all Judaea, and in Samaria, and unto the uttermost part of the earth.

What the Scripture actually says when read carefully and in context: is when you are saved, you will receive the gift of the Holy Spirit. The gift of the Spirit given to help us live a righteous lifestyle, a Torah observant lifestyle.

It is very important as we look at the gifts of the Spirit in Scripture that we interpret correctly what is being said. Misunderstanding or relating out of context, scriptures pertaining to the gifts will give a wrong and confusing view of what God wants from us. We must look at the Scripture and see what type of gift is being spoken of.

- Is it talking about Spiritual gifts *(the gifts operated by the Spirit)*

- The gift of the Spirit *(the Spirit itself as a gift)*
- Gifts and talents that we naturally have.
- How would a first century Jewish believer have understood what was said.

As long as we keep these things in mind when we are interpreting, we should come to a logical and correct view of what the Spirit and the Word are helping us to understand. I say "logical" because faith does not mean we throw our brains out the window. We are to renew our minds to a new way of thinking and understanding. Not to just accept any doctrine and be blown about by the wind in what we believe.

Corinthian Fellowship

Corinth was a port and trade city which had 1000's passing through weekly.

As the congregation grew, it was becoming a mix of Jew and gentile. Many of these gentiles had perverted ideas of morality and were finding it difficult to reconcile what they had learnt all their life with the changes required of them through Yeshua *(not much different today)*.

This was causing many problems within the congregation. The outside world was being brought into the fellowship; the gentiles were trying to reconcile their pre-existent beliefs with these teachings in the Torah. They were at times resisting and rejecting the Judaic background of the faith despite the Jewish leaders trying to show them otherwise. Paul had to write increasingly stronger letters to them rebuking their behaviour and explaining their errors to them.

> 1 Corinthians 3:1 KJV
> And I, brethren, could not speak unto you as unto spiritual, but as unto carnal, even as unto babes in Christ.
> 1 Corinthians KJV 3:2 I have fed you with milk, and not with meat: for hitherto ye were not able to bear it, neither yet now are ye able.
> 1 Corinthians KJV 3:3 for ye are yet carnal: for whereas there is among you envying, and strife, and divisions, are ye not carnal, and walk as men?

The congregation was struggling with adultery, who they thought was the better teacher etc. They were not walking in righteousness, nor were they glorifying God in their behaviour. Paul says clearly here in Chapter 3 verses 1-3 that he is now talking to them about the carnal issues because they are unfit to hear the spiritual. Going back to the beginning of Corinthians shows why he considers them lacking and in disarray.

> 1 Corinthians 1:12 KJV Now this I say, that every one of you saith, I am of Paul; and I of Apollos; and I of Cephas; and I of Christ.
> 1 Corinthians 1:13 KJV Is Christ divided? Was Paul crucified for you? Or were ye baptized in the name of Paul?
> 1 Corinthians 1:14 KJV I thank God that I baptized none of you, but Crispus and Gaius;

Paul was so disturbed by their behavior that he was pleased that he hadn't been the one to baptise them.

Paul spent much time reproaching them for their behavior and was pointing them back to the truth. We must also realize that in the writing of this letter Paul addresses the two groups, Jews and gentiles, in different ways. Some things he is pointing out to the gentiles specifically as it was their understanding that was wrong. Not the teaching of the Jewish believing leaders.

One of the areas they were having problems with amongst others was the "things of the Spirit", not "Gifts of the Spirit". Let me explain.

Let us look at what Paul said to them: IN CONTEXT and History to try and help them understand. Remember this was a fellowship that needed to return to the milk. They were nowhere ready for the meat or deeper meaning of the Scripture, let alone great power and the manifestations of the Spirit.. Let us look at why:

> 1 Corinthians 12:1 KJV now concerning spiritual *gifts*[5], brethren, I would not have you ignorant.
> *(Words in Italics are added words by translators; they are not in the Greek manuscripts).*

Paul at this juncture did not want to talk to them about Spiritual *gifts*: he wanted to talk to them about Spiritual <u>issues</u>. *(Mat 22:29 KJV Jesus answered and said unto them, ye do err, not knowing the Scriptures, nor the power of God.)*

> 1 Corinthians 12:2 KJV ye know that ye were <u>gentiles</u>, carried away unto these dumb idols, even as ye were led.

Notice that Paul is now aiming his rebuke at the grafted in gentiles and not the Jewish leaders and believers who he was addressing at various other times in his letters.

---

[5]   Words in *italics* in the KJV are added by the translators who believed that they finished or completed the sentence. These words are not in the original manuscripts and therefore are not <u>GOSPEL</u>

1 Corinthians CJB 12:3 wherefore I give you to understand, that no man speaking by the Spirit of God calleth Yeshua accursed: and that no man can say that Yeshua is the Lord, but by the Holy Ghost.

Paul is going back to basics here. He is explaining to them again that unless you have the Spirit of God, your eyes cannot even be opened to see the truth. Again, something the Jews understood but the gentiles had to be taught. Remember the gentiles had no pre-existent knowledge of the Spirit or the teachings of God (His Torah) or His work with the Jews throughout history.

1 Corinthians KJV 12:4 now there are diversities of gifts, but the same Spirit.

Paul is now stating a fact: there are various gifts, but these are given by the same Spirit by which they were saved. They come from nowhere else. He is starting to explain the basics again. Remember, many of these gentiles had ideas of their own about spiritual gifts because of the gods they previously worshiped. Many had seen false signs and wonders demonstrated by the priests of these religions. He is pointing them back to Adonai, the one true God.

1 Corinthians 12:5 KJV and there are differences of administrations, but the same Lord.

This can also be read as 'distinct ministries of the Spirit' but only through Yeshua. This is pointed out because the gentiles grafted in had their own pagan ideas as to what the gifts and Spirit might be. Paul is stating categorically that there is ONLY ONE true God, Spirit and Messiah.

> 1 Corinthians 12:6 KJV and there are diversities of operations, but it is the same God which worketh all in all.

There are various workings of the Spirit, but again reminds them: there is only one God by whom these will work.

- In the three preceding verses Paul is again reiterating the doctrine of the Trinity (more basics)
- Gifts are attributed to the Holy Spirit, 1 Corinthians 12:4.
- Administrations to the Lord Yeshua, 1 Corinthians 12:5.
- Operations to God the Father, 1 Corinthians 12:6.
- The Spirit always points upwards, never inwards to us. It cannot. We are of a sinful nature. Man's heart is evil continually. The Spirit can only point to Perfection and we are not that.
  1 Corinthians 12:7 KJV but the manifestation of the Spirit is given to every man to profit withal.

The Spirit will operate the gifts to profit us or educate us, leading us into a deeper relationship with the Messiah. In other words 'the meat'. However, how can you have the meat when you can't seem to grasp the milk! The very basics of the faith.

First we must notice that Paul is not saying at the beginning of chapter 12 'Spiritual Gifts' but is discussing the Spiritual state of the fellowship. He then goes on to point out again to the gentiles the basics of the faith again. Stating that, the Holy Spirit only points to the full Godhead, salvation, and nothing else. You cannot even call Yeshua Lord unless you are lead by this specific Spirit.

Having defined this Paul then moves onto the Spiritual Gifts, what they are and how they work.

The Gifts of the Spirit

Paul now starts to clarify what each gift is and what it is for. Not only that, he makes it clear that no man owns or operates these gifts as that can lead to boasting and pride. Rather he points out that the gifts are purely operated by the Spirit as He wills and not us.[6]

Let us start with the "Word of wisdom" – this is the ability to reason wisely.

This is the complete opposite of the pagans who would have you believe their faith by force: either physical or emotional and try to convince you to believe by their clever arguments. Paul had wisdom as he reasoned daily with the Jews. He did not argue with them. (*See 1 Corinthians 1:17*) He preached to them with Scriptures – the wisdom of God. Not man's wisdom. *(Acts 17:2 KJV)*

> 1 Corinthians 1:19 KJV for it is written, I will destroy the wisdom of the wise, and will bring to nothing the
> understanding of the prudent.
> 1 Corinthians 1:20 KJV Where is the wise? Where is the scribe? Where is the disputer of this world? Hath not God made foolish the wisdom of this world?
> 1 Corinthians 1:21 KJV for after that in the wisdom of God the world by wisdom knew

---

[6] "1 Corinthians 12:11 KJV" But all these worketh that one and the selfsame Spirit, dividing to every man severally as he will.

not God, it pleased God by the foolishness of preaching to save them that believe.

1 Corinthians 1:22 KJV For the Jews require a sign, and the Greeks seek after wisdom:

1 Corinthians 1:23 KJV But we preach Christ crucified, unto the Jews a stumbling block, and unto the Greeks foolishness;

1 Corinthians 1:24 KJV But unto them which are called, both Jews and Greeks, Christ the power of God, and the wisdom of God.

Verse 1:24 above is an important scripture in our relationship to the Messiah and Israel. "But unto them which are called, both Jews and Greeks". (It is a reference to Galatians and the One New Man[7] being grafted in, demonstrating Adonai sees no difference between Jew and gentile once they believe). As gentiles we are grafted into the faith of Yeshua, true biblical Judaism. Not to be confused with rabbinic Judaism.

Paul had already explained earlier in this same letter what he means. He is now reiterating it. Remember he is now speaking to the gentiles specifically, who are trying to understand theologically. Paul is saying: the wisdom you have brought in is nothing: 'leave it out guys'. It is now the Wisdom of God you need to be looking to.

The Spirit will prompt us to give instruction or direction to believers, but only through God's Word. The Bible is complete; therefore all we need to know is contained therein.

---

[7]   Ephesians 2:15

2 Timothy 3:16 KJV All Scripture is given by inspiration of God, and is profitable for doctrine, for reproof, for correction, for instruction in righteousness

Remember the Scriptures spoken of by Paul in his writing to Timothy are what we today call the Old Testament; the New is only just getting pieced together as these letters were written. Paul's information comes from what has already been written throughout history *(The Scripture already written – the Tenach)*, but understood by the Spirit. If this were not the case the New Testament and Paul's letters would contradict the Tenach. We understand through the History of what has already been written.

It is also very important to note another scripture just referenced:

1 Corinthians 1:22 KJV For the Jews require a sign, and the Greeks seek after wisdom:

This is an important scripture because it demonstrates the differences between Greek and Judaic thought. I mention this because today we are brought up in the Greek way of thinking which differs quite dramatically from the Judaic way.

Our whole world view, critical thinking, logic and biblical systematic theology are based upon Greek thinking. It is from the philosophers of the past (Plato, Socrates) that this form of thinking about the world and life, both physical and spiritual is derived. This is what this scripture is warning about. You could say that as Greek hellenised Christians we tend to understand everything with a nice neat theological bow tying everything up nicely.

Yet the Judaic thought is "we need a sign or we need to see to be able to understand". This is why God has so consistently throughout history given miraculous signs. "When we see it we will believe it". Of course we know these signs were often forgotten again pretty quickly, but that doesn't negate the different perspective taken on understanding what God means in His word.

We must remember that the scriptures were written by Jews with a Judaic mindset to a people and society that God Himself created and called His own. If we try to appropriate the word and transfer it to a Greek way of thinking we will invariably come across problems. The New Testament is written as a Jewish book. It is full of Jewish idioms written in Greek and it is this that has caused so much confusion and division amongst theologians.

The Manifestations of the Gifts

Hebrews 2:4 KJV God also bearing them witness, both with signs and wonders, and with diverse miracles, and gifts of the Holy Ghost, according to **his own will?** *(Emphasis mine)*

"1 Corinthians 12:11 KJV" But all these worketh that one and the selfsame Spirit, dividing to every man severally as he will.

God performs the Signs and Wonders and all the gifts of the Spirit by His Will, when He chooses, not when we choose. He does this as a witness of and to Himself.

1 Corinthians 12:9 KJV to another faith[8] by the same Spirit; to another the gifts of healing by the same Spirit;

To another faith — Faith is not purely abstract. If we look at the translations used for faith: we will see that faith is a practical thing.

---

[8]   G4102
πὺστις
pistis
pis'-tis

From G3982; *persuasion*, that is, *credence*; moral *conviction* (of *religious* truth, or the truthfulness of God or a religious teacher), especially *reliance* upon Christ for salvation; abstractly *constancy* in such profession; by extension the system of religious (Gospel) *truth* itself: - assurance, belief, believe, faith, fidelity.

Faith is: persuasion, credence, conviction, the truth of a teacher, assurance, belief, believe, faith, fidelity. Faith is also trust:

1 Trusting is being confident of what we hope for, convinced about things we do not see.
2 It was for this that Scripture attested the merit of the people of old.
3 By trusting, we understand that the universe was created through a spoken word of God, so that what is seen did not come into being out of existing phenomena.
4 By trusting, Hevel (Abel) offered a greater sacrifice than Kayin (Cain); because of this, he was attested as righteous, with God giving him this testimony on the ground of his gifts. Through having trusted, he still continues to speak, even though he is dead.
5 By trusting, Hanokh (Enoch) was taken away from this life without seeing death - "He was not to be found, because God took him away" - for he has been attested as having been, prior to being taken away, well pleasing to God.
6 And without trusting, it is impossible to be well pleasing to God, because whoever approaches him must trust that he does exist and that he becomes a Rewarder to those who seek him out.

Faith is strength, faith is not something intangible, it is real. Faith is trusting in the truth. Faith in God gives us the ability to teach the truth. Faith in God brings the assurance of our salvation and the strength and conviction to share it with others.

When we say: we will step out in faith, what we are saying is: we will step out in the strength of God of whom our faith is in. As the Lord has us 'step out' into various 'ventures', He will strengthen us for the task. He will give us the faith to see through what has been started. What He has started through us. This is done by His Spirit thus glorifying God. Paul has already given this example by the way he was living his life.

Some are asked to step out into areas that need a lot of strength, maybe even to death.

Also faith and healing are placed together. This is not accidental. It is not faith that will heal someone who is sick nor their faith that will heal them. It is God who will heal by His Spirit. It is His strength that will heal not our own. Not our faith. If our faith was sufficient *(our strength, assurance etc)* we would not need more strength for a task given to us by the Holy Spirit.

When teachers, ministers or pastors say to you: "you are not healed because you don't have enough faith" they are turning something God does to glorify Himself onto man's own ability through his own faith. If man had the faith to heal himself, we would not need God.

Are there an exceptions to this rule?

Matthew 9:22 KJV But Yeshua turned him about, and when he saw her, he said, Daughter, be of good comfort; thy faith hath made thee whole. And the woman was made whole from that hour.

Matthew 9:29 KJV then touched he their eyes, saying, According to your faith be it unto you.

Luke 17:6 KJV And the Lord said, if ye had faith as a grain of mustard seed, ye might say unto this sycamore tree, be thou plucked up by the root, and be thou planted in the sea; and it should obey you.

The question here is: was the faith that Yeshua was speaking of the spiritual faith that they had in the ability to be healed? Or was it the faith they had in God that had or could heal them?

What's the difference?

The difference may be a subtle one, but the onus is on who gets the Glory that is changed.

If your faith is in the ability to be healed based on your own faith because you have faith in your faith, then you are placing the onus in the wrong place. This is giving man the power to heal, perhaps using the name of Jesus as a magic word or incantation to bring about what you believe or prefer to believe. In this case it is through us this operation is performed *(sinful people)*, not the Spirit. So it cannot be faith in the act of healing that is spoken of in these scriptures.

It is faith in the ability of the giver of the gift.

The faith we are to have is faith in God, not in the healing.

All things must point to God and the Godhead; as soon as we point to ourselves in any way as regards the gifts we add sin into the equation. God does not operate in sin. He is Holy. God by His Spirit directs us away from sin and encourages us to look at the creator as the supplier of all things and not at the supply.

Yeshua said:

Mark 11:22 KJV And Jesus answering saith unto them, Have faith in God.

He said have faith in God and these things will happen. He did not say have faith that these things will happen. Let your strength be in and from God only, then He is glorified and not us. FAITH ALWAYS POINTS TO GOD

Next we read in Scripture about the gifts of Healing – there are 2 types of healing. Note that it is always translated Gifts[9] of Healing and not gift of healing: There is the physical and the emotional.

Although the Greek χάρισμα (Charisma) appears to be in the singular, it is also the plural as the Greek there is differentiation between the two

---

[9]   G5486

χάρισμα

charisma

char'-is-mah

From G5483; a (divine) *gratuity,* that is, *deliverance* (from danger or
     passion); (specifically) a (spiritual) *endowment,* that is,
     (subjectively) religious *qualification,* or (objectively) miraculous
     faculty: - (free) gift.

other than the context of the sentence. Always translated here in the plural in all biblical translations. Thus we have *Gifts of Healing*.

One of the ministries of believers is to help the poor and the widowed.

These need healing, nurturing and love to guide them from the pain and stress of the situation they are in; the same with other believers, we all have pain in our past. *(Confess your sins one to another; bring to light that which is in darkness).*

The Lord will use this gift through people who have a love for people and a desire to help others *(it is also a natural gifting)*. We should all be like this, but in reality some can empathise better than others, which is why the Lord operates the gifts through us all differently. And also, remember that the gifts are given to unify the body and not to divide it; this is what Paul, in my opinion, has been saying overall:

> *"Don't you understand even the basics; you are meant to be helping each other not contending with each other. God's Spirit brings unity amongst believers to glorify God. There will be division enough between believers and unbelievers. Surely this is bad enough. But by your childish behaviour and lack of understanding you're dividing the congregation; you're trying to run before you can walk. Leave the teachings you had before behind. You need a new understanding now. Through the renewing of your minds, all that worship stuff you had before is nothing. Why*

are you bringing it here. Now be quiet and listen while I tell you again" (My Paraphrase)

He is attempting to get the people to refocus their opinions and lifestyle around what Adonai has declared as righteous and develop themselves into a cohesive group that is sharing the gifts. Thus allowing them to harmonize their lives together. In so doing they are living correctly and glorifying God, as opposed to being selfish and prideful.

The physical healings are a manifestation of the Spirit as He wills and not as we choose. If we had the gift to heal people as and when we chose we would be seen as no more than the faith healers. People would be looking to the man. The glory must always go to God, never man.

Whereas, the gift of healing emotional struggles using Scripture *(not Psychiatry or Psychology)* shows the work of the Spirit in our life and again glorifies God.

Remember, the manifest signs *(The signs that can be seen to have a physical and miraculous action)* follow the preaching of the Gospel and are a witness to the unbelievers, not the believers. Whereas the emotional healing profits all.

Mark 16:20 KJV and they went forth, and preached everywhere, the Lord working with them, and confirming the word with signs following. Amen.

The reason we do not see many genuine healings today is because the so called "Great

Men of God" claim to have *(possess/own)* the gift of physical healings from God. They then put on great shows where 10's of 1000's turn up to see healings. Sadly these people are coming to see the "great man of God", the show and the healings. They are not given the Gospel of salvation after which these signs will follow, but are taught that you are healed by faith. God has in effect become secondary to the process. Faith is taught as man's strength and by his ability to have faith he is healed. The Gospel message is abbreviated to a message of faith and not salvation and repentance through Yeshua by His Spirit and His atoning work of the cross. Faith itself becomes the gospel.

> 1 Corinthians 12:10 KJV *(part 1)* to another the working of miracles[10]; to another prophecy; to another discerning of spirits; to another...

The word for miracles here is 'Dunamis' and not the Hebrew word 'Pala'[11] – this word apart

---

[10]   G1411 δυἰναμις dunamis *doo'-nam-is*
From G1410; *force* (literally or figuratively); specifically miraculous *power* (usually by implication a *miracle* itself): - ability, abundance, meaning, might (-ily, -y, -y deed), (worker of) miracle (-s), power, strength, violence, mighty (wonderful) work.

[11]   H6381
פָּלָא pâlâ' *paw-law'*
A primitive root; properly perhaps to *separate*, that is, *distinguish* (literally or figuratively); by implication to *be* (causatively *make*) *great, difficult, wonderful:* - accomplish, (arise . . . too, be too) hard, hidden, things too high, (be, do, do a, shew) marvelous (-ly, -els, things, work), miracles, perform, separate, make singular, (be, great, make) wonderful (-ers, -ly, things, works), wondrous (things, works, -ly).

from being translated as miracle is also translated as 'Strength' or 'might' or as in the following verse "Power", it is where we get the word 'Dynamo' from..

> 1 Corinthians KJV 2.4 And my speech and my preaching was not with enticing words of man's wisdom, but in demonstration of the Spirit and of <u>power</u>: *(Dunamis: this is a demonstration of the gift in use)*

Paul is giving an example to the gentile believers of what it means to walk in this power. He is showing how God will guide our speech by His Spirit as we can do nothing of ourselves. The Lord by His Spirit will speak through us. How does He do this? By giving us the strength to proclaim the Scriptures in uncertain situations. By the ability to expound the Word in power, so that the barriers are broken down. Paul has proved this in the verse prior as he tells them:

> 1 Corinthians 2:3 KJV And I was with you in weakness, and in fear, and in much trembling.

Thus demonstrating to them that they were being witnessed to through this act of such preaching in power. God had opened their eyes by this powerful preaching and by His Spirit. Everything must point to the Godhead.

An early Jewish believer would have understood what Paul was saying. He was reiterating earlier statements in his letter in a way the gentiles could comprehend.

Paul is showing them the Scriptural argument against what they were taught through the worship of Aphrodite. Remember that she was associated with the goddess of persuasion and the way of the people was to persuade through their clever arguments (wisdom).

Paul is reiterating in these verses what he has already said. The gentile background was different in understanding to the Jewish believer. Paul was speaking to them in a way they would comprehend from their understanding of power from a background of goddess worship. Paul became a Jew to the Jew and a gentile to the gentiles. He explained in the terminology the listener could relate to.

When we go back to the beginning of the letter to the Corinthians we see that Paul addressed his letter to the Jewish leaders of the congregation who it had been reported had needed his help. Remember these are Jewish believers who were not all brought up locally and had little understanding of the gentile ways. They were Jews who remained separate from these things, which was right according to the Torah. So Paul tells them how to chastise the congregation. He explains the basics to them clearly in Chapters 1-9. Because they did not understand he came back at them from a different angle. One he hoped they would understand.

1 Corinthians 9:11 KJV If we *(The Jewish Leaders)* have sown unto you spiritual things,

is it a great thing if we shall reap your *(gentile)* carnal things?

Why are you trying to corrupt the root of the faith?

They did not understand what was being explained to them. If they had understood the spiritual things they would not have persisted in promoting the carnal. They would not have continued in the way they knew. It would appear that they wanted a form of belief that suited them. Paul was telling them in no uncertain terms that they were wrong.

Matthew Henry sums it up nicely:

"While heathens, they had not been influenced by the Spirit of Christ. No man can call Christ Lord, with believing dependence upon him, unless that faith is wrought by the Holy Ghost. No man could believe with his heart, or prove by a miracle, that Yeshua was Christ, unless by the Holy Ghost. There are various gifts, and various offices to perform, but all proceed from one God, one Lord, one Spirit; that is, from the Father, Son, and Holy Ghost, the origin of all spiritual blessings. No man has them merely for himself. The more he profits others, the more will they turn to his own account. The gifts mentioned appear to mean exact understanding, and uttering the doctrines of the Christian religion; the knowledge of mysteries, and skill to give advice and counsel. Also the gift of healing the sick, the working of miracles, and to explain Scripture by a peculiar gift of the Spirit, and ability to speak and interpret languages. If we have any knowledge of the truth, or any power to make it known, we must give all the glory of God. The greater the gifts are, the more the possessor is exposed to temptations, and the larger is the measure of grace needed to keep him humble and spiritual; and he will meet with more painful experiences and humbling dispensations. We have little cause to glory in any gifts bestowed on us, or to despise those who have them not."[1]

Discerning[12] of spirits – continuing his explanation of spiritual things Paul is again telling them that they must learn, by the Spirit: the Truth. Check all things by Scripture to see if it is true. Discerning the spirit means to judge the spirit. Judge what is being said; either in the pulpit or by individuals to see whether it is of God or not. How do we do this? We look to the Word, the Scriptures. We also look at the fruit coming from those teachings. Both corporately and individually.

We cannot interpret Scripture by whether it 'feels right', or 'sits right with our spirit'. We must test everything by God's Word. Many things can 'sit right' because of who we are and what we prefer to hear. That does not make it right according to Scripture. All things must be tested.

Acts 17:10 KJV and the brethren immediately sent away Paul and Silas by night unto Berea:

---

[12]   G1253
διαὶκρισις
diakrisis
dee-ak'-ree-sis
From G1252; judicial *estimation:* - discern (-ing), disputation.

who coming thither went into the synagogue of the Jews.
Acts 17:11 KJV these were more noble than those in Thessalonica, in that they received the word with all readiness of mind, and searched the Scriptures daily, whether those things were so.

2 Timothy 2:15 KJV Study to show thyself approved unto God, a workman that needeth not to be ashamed, rightly dividing the word of truth.

Paul in his letter to Timothy sums up well what he is saying to the gentile believers:

1 Timothy 4:9 KJV Faithful is the Word and worthy of all acceptance;
1 Timothy 4:10 KJV for to this we also labour and are reproached, because we hope on the living God, who is Saviour of all men, especially of believers.
1 Timothy 4:11 KJV Enjoin and teach these things.
1 Timothy 4:12 KJV Let no one despise your youth, but become an example of the believers in word, in conduct, in love, in spirit, in faith, in purity.
1 Timothy 4:13 KJV until I come, attend to reading, to exhortation to the doctrine.
1 Timothy 4:14 KJV Do not be neglectful of the gift in you, which was given to you through prophecy *(teaching and expounding*

of Scripture), with laying on of the hands of the elder hood.

1 Timothy 4:15 KJV Give care to these things; be in these things in order that your progress may be plain in all.

1 Timothy 4:16 KJV Give attention to yourself and to the doctrine; continue in them, for doing this; you will both deliver yourself and those hearing you.

How do we know that the good doctrine our Messiah and the apostles were pointing to was the Torah?

Proverbs 4:2 KJV **For I give you good doctrine, forsake ye not my law. (Torah)**

Forget the History, Misunderstand the Scripture

1 Corinthians 12:10 KJV *(part 2)* to another ~~divers~~[13] kinds of tongues; to another the interpretation of tongues:

An important fact to note about this Scripture is the lack of the word UNKNOWN, DIVERSE or any other variation of these words appearing anywhere at any time in the original Text relating to the gifts, and especially to Tongues. The words in italics are added words. Many translations italicize the first time the word "unknown" is used in Corinthians 12 but leave it in later on in the verses and elsewhere when talking of Tongues.

However, the word "unknown" is still not in the original Greek. It has been added to allow the Gift of Tongues to mean something it doesn't. This is either done through man's basic lack of understanding by removing the Judaic Root of the meaning, or a deliberate ploy by the Devil to bring division amongst believers.

I think perhaps, the latter by deception to the former as tongues have now become an experiential form of Christianity. If Satan brings in this deception along with confusion as to what the outpouring of the Spirit is, and to whom it is for at various times, then we have even more divisive deceptions going on in the end times. A look at

---

[13]   Words Unknown or Diverse - Not in original Greek Manuscripts

how much the tongues issue has divided Christians we can see the validity of this statement.

There are many churches with ministers preaching that if you do not have the gift of tongues you can't possibly be saved as it is _The_ definitive proof of being filled with the Spirit, and thus proof that you are saved. This is turning a misunderstood verse into a doctrine of salvation. Yet as we read earlier, the definitive proof of being filled with the Spirit is our obedience to a Torah lifestyle and God's commandments.

Nowhere is the speaking of tongues taught as a proof of salvation, though it was given as a sign to the Jews to strike them to jealousy. Only by misinterpreting the out pouring of the Spirit on the Jewish believers at Pentecost and then the Baptism of the gentiles in the Spirit 10 years later at Caesarea as a sign to the Jews can this, no matter how weakly, be justified.

Throughout the history of the Nation of Israel, it never followed that there was speaking in Tongues associated with believing. Remember, it was always by the Spirit that people were and are saved. If this was a manifest sign throughout the history of salvation, then perhaps this view could be taken, but as it was not; then it still is not. Scripture supports Scripture; if it doesn't then it is an opinion.

As the Word used for Tongues[14] only indicates that it is a language naturally learnt and not that it is a language we cannot understand. We cannot legitimately try to force it to mean something it does not.

> 1 Corinthians 13:1 KJV though I speak with the tongues of men and of angels, and have not charity, I am become as sounding brass, or a tinkling cymbal.
> 1 Corinthians 13:2 KJV and though I have the gift of prophecy, and understand all mysteries, and all knowledge; and though I have all faith, so that I could remove mountains, and have not charity, I am nothing.
> 1 Corinthians 13:3 KJV and though I bestow all my goods to feed the poor, and though I give my body to be burned, and have not charity, it profiteth me nothing.

Ah look! See Paul spoke the language of angels that proves there is a heavenly Unknown language.

Does it? Remember when interpreting Scripture; what is the most important rule? Context, context, context...

---

[14]**G1100**
γλῶσσα
glōssa
gloce'-sah
Of uncertain affinity; the *tongue*; by implication a *language* (specifically one naturally unacquired): - tongue.

- Does Paul have all knowledge?
- Does he have all Faith?
- Has he given his body to be burnt?

The answer is no. He does not have and did not do any of these things. This is Paul simply showing the importance for the need for Love *(Charity)* above all else. In 1 Corinthians 15:29 Paul also talks about the "baptism of the dead", yet we know this is not a biblical practice. This is again Paul pointing out the error of the gentile pagan practices being brought in.

It is a traditional Jewish trait, especially during a teaching session to answer a question with a question. Jesus also did this regularly. The question you respond with forces the original questioner to answer his own question. In other words: the answer should be obvious or with a little thought the answer should be gleaned. Understanding the Judaic way of thinking helps us to appreciate this.

As for speaking the "language of Angels", the only language we find Angels speaking anywhere in Scripture is the languages of men speaking God's Word. If they did not speak the language of men they would not have been understood when they spoke. It is assumption that they speak a language in heaven other than one that is already on earth. In fact the only language spoken by angels in scripture is Hebrew or Aramaic, the languages of the people.

What language did Adam speak? Wouldn't God have given him a language already spoken in heaven? (Maybe Hebrew) as the language barrier was not set up until Babel.

> Genesis 11:1 KJV and the whole earth was of one language, and of one speech. (Hebrew? Maybe)

All people spoke the same language before this time. There is no reference to it being different in heaven, remember God spoke to Adam in the garden. Adam did not have to translate as God spoke to him in the language he *(Adam)* already knew. The language he was given.

The Tongues spoken at Pentecost and when the gentiles were first saved was a proof as to the reversal of Babel. At Babel God separated the languages and put up the barriers to decimate the evil ways they were living. This sign of reversal was to show that God had now opened the way for the gentiles: what He *(God)* had separated He has now reconciled. There was no Israel before Babel. There was only the remnant, as it was with Noah. Perhaps it is the remnant that continued with the language of Adam and of Heaven; after all they were still following God, so why would God confuse them. Aramaic and Hebrew are important as languages throughout history.

Assuming something in Scripture; but forgetting the History, leads to misunderstanding.

TO ANOTHER DIVERS KINDS OF TONGUES - The power of speaking various languages;

Act 2:4 KJV and they were all filled with the Holy Ghost, and began to speak with other tongues, as the Spirit gave them utterance.

Act 2:7 KJV And they were all (The Jews) amazed and marveled, saying one to another, Behold, are not all these which speak Galileans?

Act 2:8 KJV And how hear we every man in our own tongue[15], wherein we were born?

Act 2:9 KJV Parthians, and Medes, and Elamites, and the dwellers in Mesopotamia, and in Judea, and Cappadocia, in Pontus, and Asia,

Act 2:10 KJV Phrygia, and Pamphylia, in Egypt, and in the parts of Libya about Cyrene, and strangers of Rome, Jews and proselytes,

Act 2:11 KJV Cretes and Arabians, we do hear them speak in our tongues the wonderful works of God.

As can be seen by these Scriptures, it would appear that not all spoke in the same Tongue. Some spoke Egyptian others Arabic etc. This is the Spirit imparting the gift as He will and not as we choose. And what were they speaking? They were speaking the "Wonderful Works of God" in the

---

[15]   G1258

διαìλεκτος

dialektos

dee-al'-ek-tos

From G1256; a (mode of) discourse, that is, "dialect": -
    language, tongue.

Max Debono-De-Laurentis

languages understood by those around them. Not something unknown. Nor a heavenly language not understood by man. But as stated by those around them, a language that was clearly understood. This glorified God. The most amazing part to the listeners at this time was that this was coming specifically from Galileans who were considered by many to be uneducated. So how was this happening? (Acts 2:7)

The Spirit always points to the Godhead, never man.

1 Corinthians 14:29 KJV and *if there are*[16] two or three prophets[17], let them speak, and let the others discern.

This verse says with authority: two or three prophets, not as implied with the addition of the words: 'if there were'. In other words: Let the inspired speaker or teachers speak what is to be the interpretation of the Scripture and then let the others judge the truth of that interpretation. In other words *(Discern)*; Does it tie up with what the rest of Scripture says? If not then reject it. If

---

[16]   Words added by translators – Not in original Manuscripts

[17]   G4396
προφῆὶτης
prophetes
prof-ay'-tace
From a compound of G4253 and G5346; a foreteller ("prophet"); by analogy an inspired speaker; by extension a poet: - prophet.

none can expound on the Word, be silent. The Spirit is not speaking at this time. No Scripture is for personal interpretation. All these gifts come together to edify the body in teaching and understanding. Not amazingly powerful displays of God inspired power. Remember about what Paul is talking to them. He is rebuking them.

It is important to recognize the differences between the two types of tongues spoken of in Scripture. There was, as just discussed, the sign to the Jews, but then there is another type of tongue, a different type spoken of in Corinthians.

What are the other Tongues spoken of in Corinthians all about?

We need to understand traditional Jewish history to answer this question. Again, knowing the tradition helps us to clarify the understanding.

There was a system in place in the Synagogues of reading the Scriptures in a particular way, this was called Targum.

Targum

To "Targum"[18] is to interpret, the term is usually used specifically in the translation of the Bible into Aramaic from the original Hebrew and then expounded by someone who is given

---

[18]Tar·gum (tär-goom)

n. Any of several Aramaic explanatory translations or paraphrasing of the Hebrew Scriptures.

revelation and understanding as to the meaning of that scripture. According to an ancient Jewish tradition, the public reading of the Bible in the synagogue must be accompanied by a reading in Hebrew, a translation into Aramaic, which was the spoken language of most Jews in Israel and Babylonia during the Talmudic era; this would include the believing Jewish leaders at Corinth.

The normal practice was that after each portion was read from the written scroll in Hebrew, an official known as the "Turgeman" or "Meturgeman" would then recite orally an Aramaic rendering of the passage. *(And then speak in tongues – or translate to the common language of the fellowship).* In Corinth this would have been predominantly Greek. This was the regular practice at the time. It was the accepted tradition therefore not specifically mentioned in the Scriptures. It was understood by the Jews that this was the way things were done. The gentiles had to be taught to understand this.

As the use of Aramaic declined, this practice of reciting the Scripture in the synagogue fell into disuse in most Jewish communities. However, this practice can still be found in the synagogues of few Jews left in the Yemen today. They read the Scriptures in Hebrew, speak them into Aramaic, and then translate them into the language of the people. In this case Arabic. They would then be Targumed (expounded).

What was being explained to the gentiles was the tradition of reading from the Scriptures and then Targum or Interpret those Scriptures, not just by translation but interpretation: e.g. what does it mean in relation to us and our relationship with God? Tongues and interpretation must go together or else no one is edified.

There would definitely be translation in the congregation, but interpreting is something we wait upon the Spirit for. e.g. what does this mean? What is God saying to us? How do we expound these Scriptures just read? Yeshua went to the Synagogues and interpreted *(He would Targum)* the Scriptures to the listeners; He would read them in Hebrew, translate them into Aramaic and then explain what the Scriptures were saying with authority. Anyone can read Scripture but it is only by the Spirit that we can understand it.

This is where we come in with the understanding of what is being explained to the Corinthians. Remember again, Paul is explaining the basics to them. Many of them were trying to give interpretations to the Scriptures by their own knowledge *(Wisdom)* and not by the Spirit of God. Paul is telling them throughout this letter to forget what they had before and renew their minds to conform to the correct teaching.

"Unknown Tongues" is something that many cults and worshipers of foreign gods and Satanists do on a regular basis. Also known as *'Ecstatic Utterances'*. These are meant to show that they are in communication and communion with their god.

This is not a counterfeit of the Corinthian Tongues. It is however a perversion of the miraculous languages spoken at Pentecost and Caesarea. The devil will not copy what God is doing, as a copy is the same thing. He perverts what the Lord is doing in order to deceive.

A truth is only the truth until a lie is mixed in. After that the truth is no longer the truth. A lie with a little truth is still a lie, as is a truth with a little lie. There are no 'white lies'. God's Word is true. Any deviation, no matter how small is a perversion of the Word and is therefore a lie.

Our Lord and Saviour will always do things decently and in order. Satan on the other hand brings in confusion and destruction through deception. He is the father of lies. (John 8:44)

Let us examine some of the other Scriptures relating to 'Tongues' and see which type of Tongues they are referring to.

> Mark 16:15 KJV and he said unto them, Go ye into all the world, and preach the gospel to every creature.
> Mark 16:16 KJV He that believeth and is baptized shall be saved; but he that believeth not shall be damned.
> Mark 16:17 KJV and these signs shall follow them that believe; in my name shall they cast out devils; they shall speak with new tongues;
> Mark 16:18 KJV they shall take up serpents; and if they drink any deadly thing, it shall not hurt them; they shall lay hands on the sick, and they shall recover.

The key verse here is Mark 16:15, they are to go into "all the world" and preach, how can this be done without learning new languages? "They shall speak with new tongues". (Mark 16:17)

Yeshua said that certain signs will follow those that preached the Gospel. Notice again that signs always follow the preaching of the Gospel. They do not precede the preaching. Unless it is the gift of Tongues or preaching the Gospel miraculously in another language. The ability to preach the Gospel in a language you have not learned; and what is this sign for? It is a sign to the unbeliever that the Testimony you are giving is in truth inspired by God through His Spirit. It is also aimed at the unbelieving Jews to provoke them to jealousy. This happening in the temple at Pentecost would have spread amongst the nation of Israel like wildfire and then when they saw this sign it would be a confirmation of what they had heard.

This testifies of God and Glorifies Him. This also meant that the Word was spread further afield far more quickly. Later new languages would need to be learnt to give the Gospel message to the speakers of those languages. It may be that the language learnt is spiritually given as a sign rather than the laborious task of learning it by rote.

Both of these glorify God. Learning a new language is difficult, but despite that, the Spirit will allow the gospel message to be given into that language to be accurate.

Acts 19:6 KJV and when Paul had laid his hands upon them, the Holy Ghost came on them; and they spake with tongues, and prophesied.

As we have seen previously they will speak under the inspiration of God the message of Truth by the Holy Spirit and they did this in various languages.

1 Corinthians 12:28 KJV And God hath set some in the church, first apostles, secondarily prophets, thirdly teachers, after that miracles, then gifts of healings, helps, governments, diversities of tongues.

As we examine Corinthians we note that all the above are designed and designated by God to edify, teach and chastise the Church where necessary. This is what Paul was saying to the Corinthian Church: *'Get your act together people. Leave your pagan, carnal ways behind and seek after the truth, by God's Spirit and not your own understanding'*.

1 Corinthians 12:30 KJV Have all the gifts of healing? Do all speak with tongues? Do all interpret?

The above Scripture asks the question: Do we have all these things? The answer is "no". The Lord by His Spirit gives these things as He wills for His glory, not ours. Therefore not all people can speak in tongues. We know that is correct in this context because not all could read Hebrew and

Aramaic. Does the Spirit give all the ability to interpret or teach the Word, again no.

> 1 Corinthians 13:8 KJV Charity never faileth: but whether there be prophecies, they shall fail; whether there be tongues, they shall cease; whether there be knowledge, it shall vanish away.

This verse says that these gifts will fade away. Which makes sense, as once the Scriptures and message has been translated into all languages, we would no longer need this gift. That is not to say the Lord would not use it from time to time. It does however state that it will not be in common use. It will fade away as it is no longer needed. This shows that in both aspects of the Tongues spoken of it will fade away, as only the Jews of the Yemen still use the Tongues and Interpretation mentioned in Corinthians.

> 1 Corinthians 14:5 KJV I would that ye all spake with tongues, but rather that ye prophesied: for greater is he that prophesieth than he that speaketh, with tongues, except he interpret, that the church may receive edifying.

This is a clear explanation of Targum and teaching under the inspiration of God. This is all for the edification of the Church. If we could all speak and understand the Hebrew or Aramaic it would be better, there would be no need to interpret. But we cannot, so it is preferable for us to understand and interpret what is read so that we can edify the body with correct teaching under the inspiration of the Spirit. Notice how all these gifts are placed together, this is because they are all to do with teaching and the edification of the body; yet tongues in other places is for the unbeliever.

> 1 Corinthians 14:6 KJV Now, brethren, if I come unto you speaking with tongues, what shall I profit you, except I shall speak to you either by revelation *(Discernment)*, or by knowledge *(Understanding)*, or by prophesying *(Teaching under Inspiration)*, or by doctrine *(Torah)*?

What is the point of me speaking Hebrew to you if you do not understand it? It is better if I come in straight away with the interpretation, the discerned meaning, the teaching and understanding of the scripture you need in your own language. Paul is still admonishing them.

> 1 Corinthians 14:13 KJV wherefore let him that speaketh in an ~~unknown~~ tongue pray that he may interpret.
> 1 Corinthians 14:14 KJV for if I pray in an ~~unknown~~ tongue, my spirit prayeth, but my understanding is unfruitful.
> 1 Corinthians 14:15 KJV what is it then? I will pray with the spirit, and I will pray with the understanding also: I will sing with the spirit, and I will sing with the understanding also.

1 Corinthians 14:16 KJV Else when thou shalt bless with the spirit, how shall he that occupieth the room of the <u>unlearned</u> say Amen at thy giving of thanks, seeing he understandeth not what thou sayest?

1 Corinthians 14:17 KJV for thou verily givest thanks well, but the other is not edified.

1 Corinthians 14:18 KJV I thank my God, I speak with tongues more than ye all: (I'm Multilingual)

1 Corinthians 14:19 KJV yet in the church I had rather speak five words with my understanding, that by my voice I might teach others also, than ten thousand words in an unknown tongue. (Speak the language you understand than one I would prefer)

1 Corinthians 14:20 KJV Brethren, be not children in understanding: howbeit in malice be ye children, but in understanding be men.

As in Messianic congregations and Synagogues today, prayers would be learnt in Hebrew. They would be memorized and all would pray together. Just as the SHEMA[19] is recited in the synagogues and Messianic Fellowships in Hebrew. Being able to repeat the prayers or Shema parrot fashion does not mean you know the translation. What is the point of doing this if you cannot translate what is said?

---

[19] Deuteronomy 6:4 KJV Hear, O Israel: The LORD our God is one LORD:
Deuteronomy 6:5 KJV And thou shalt love the LORD thy God with all thine heart, and with all thy soul, and with all thy might.

God knows what you are saying as does the Spirit, but no one else is edified. The Unlearned, those that have not learnt the language could not agree with your prayer as he could not understand it. We are to stand together and in agreement in prayer. We cannot agree with what we have not understand.

Baruch Ata Adonai, Elohenu Melech Ha'olam, Hamatsi Lechem Mim Ha'aretz Amen

This is a prayer in Hebrew. If the prayer is prayed and someone who hasn't learnt Hebrew is present, they cannot agree unless it is translated. "Yet this is giving thanks well".

For all the other person knows I could have said: "God is a pygmy in a little pink dress, Amen

How could they agree?

What it does say though is:

Blessed art thou O Lord our God, King of the Universe, who brings forth Bread from the Earth.

Understanding the English *(or your Tongue)* you could perhaps agree with the prayer, not otherwise. Hence the need for a Meturgeman or translator. In modern terms, we often see a preacher preaching to the congregation with an interpreter proclaiming in another language what the preacher is saying. That language may be

Spanish, French, English or even for the deaf with sign language.

> 1 Corinthians 14:22 KJV wherefore tongues are for a sign, not to them that believe, but to them that believe not: but prophesying serveth not for them that believe not, but for them which believe.
>
> 1 Corinthians 14:23 KJV If therefore the whole church be come together into one place, and all speak with tongues, and there come in those that are unlearned, or unbelievers, will they not say that ye are mad?

Either these last two verses written together contradict each other as regards tongues, or these last two verses show the difference between the two tongues. The first is for believers and the second for unbelievers. The first is a language understood by men of other nations giving glory to God. The second is for the edification of the Church by understanding the Scripture in a local language rather than Hebrew or Aramaic.

There is a distinction between the two types of tongue in Scripture. To join them together as one, and to make them mean the same thing is at best a misunderstanding and at worst a deliberate attempt to undermine the teaching of Scripture, Biblical history and understanding of the basics of Judaism and hence the root of our faith.

What we do see today though is that believers are so focused on what Spiritual gift they have. Whether they are a prophet or apostle, that they are too busy to spend time studying what God is really saying. They have become so focused on self and what makes them feel good that they have forgotten that they are to focus upward toward Yeshua and not on self. Rather die to self. Satan "prowls around seeking whom he may devour" and today's Christians seem more than happy to be gobbled up.

The Offices granted by the Spirit

Did you know all the Apostles were Jewish? There were no gentile Apostles.

> 1 Corinthians 12:28 KJV And God hath set some in the church, first apostles[20], secondarily prophets, thirdly teachers, after that miracles, then gifts of healings, helps, governments, diversities of tongues.

Remember in Paul's letter he is still admonishing and explaining to the Corinthian gentiles the basics of the faith and how things are meant to operate. They were trying to promote from their own wisdom and ideas as opposed to the correct biblical and traditional Judaic format.

Paul is making the point to the gentiles that Apostles are first in importance and need to be heeded. He does not state that there will be more Apostles. These Apostles were sent out personally by Yeshua to instruct and initiate the believers

---

[20]

G652
ἀπόστολος
apostolos
ap-os'-tol-os
From G649; a delegate; specifically an ambassador of the Gospel; officially a commissioner of Christ ("apostle"), (with miraculous powers): - apostle, messenger, he that is sent.

and doctrine in its early stages. This is what Paul is doing by writing this letter, and by the fact that we are reading this letter, shows that they were trusted and sent directly by Yeshua, and that they achieved the purpose for which they were sent.

When we read the letter and comprehend that Paul is speaking directly to the gentiles at this point we can put what Paul is saying into its correct context. He is not explaining to the world at large that more Apostles will follow, but stating categorically that the Apostles sent by Yeshua should be heeded. Christ sent them out for a purpose. Personally. Paul is still admonishing and instructing the gentiles.

An Apostle is an ambassador. An ambassador can only be appointed and sent out by the person in charge of a country. Only a president, prime minister, king or queen can appoint one. They are not democratically elected by the 'underlings'. Even the boss of a company would make sure that the person he is sending out to represent his company is up to the job. He would personally send out people he trusted. If someone is in a position to instruct the 'underlings' on the policy of the company and make those policies clear for the worker, they need to be trusted and well instructed in the company way. They must also be in regular communication with the boss.

The Jewish equivalent is the Shli'ach or "sent one". He was an authorized Jewish emissary who officially represented a synagogue. He would perform acts of legal significance for the benefit of the synagogue and not himself. Nothing new, but the continuation of a regular practice that is ongoing to this day in some Messianic and orthodox synagogues.

> Galatians 1:1 KJV Paul, an apostle, (not of men, neither by man, but by Yeshua Christ, and God the Father, who raised him from the dead)

Paul further points out that he is the Apostle to the gentiles, which was his appointment. He was specifically commissioned to do this, by Yeshua. That is why we see his letters in Scripture when referring to the gentiles. *(Corinthians, Romans etc.)*

> Romans 11:13 KJV For I speak to you gentiles, inasmuch as I am the apostle of the gentiles, I magnify mine office:

He points out that he was not made an Apostle to the Jews because of what he was prior to his salvation. He was the chief persecutor of the Jewish believers. He was also a very well trained Rabbi and respected amongst the orthodox Pharisees. He was originally one of those Yeshua had called dogs and swine.

> 1 Corinthians 9:1 KJV Am I not an apostle? Am I not free? have I not seen Jesus Christ our Lord? Are not ye my work in the Lord?
> 1 Corinthians 9:2 KJV If I be not an apostle unto others, yet doubtless I am to you: for

the seal of mine apostleship are ye in the Lord. *(Talking to the gentiles)*

1 Corinthians 15:9 KJV For I am the least of the apostles, that am not meet to be called an apostle, because I persecuted the church of God. *(Not gentile believers but Jewish believers. He was not concerned at that time with what the gentiles believed)*

1 Timothy 2:7 KJV Whereunto I am ordained a preacher, and an apostle, (I speak the truth in Christ, *and* lie not) a teacher of the gentiles in faith and verity.

There is no mention in scripture of New Apostles being sent out. Only disciples.

- Are all these apostles today claiming that Jesus spoke to them?
- Personally appointed them?
- Given them the same permissions and abilities to understand scripture as the Jewish Apostles?
- Are there any gentile Apostles in Scripture?
- Did Jesus personally tell them they are to be apostles and to set Halachah or doctrine and policy?
- Do they fully understand Scripture from a Judaic background and interpretation?
- Do they know the Judaic customs and expound the root?

There can be no more Apostles. Those that claim to be apostles today are appointing a title to themselves or each other based on man's sending forth and not Gods by direct appointment through Yeshua.

If it were the case that these men are being sent out: why is it that all the modern apostles preach contrary to Scripture? Why are they setting Church policy that leads people away from the truth? e.g Rejecting Torah!

An Apostle was a high position and one no one should want. If you are directly responsible for helping to lead the believers into truth, you will be judged much stricter by what you teach.

> Luke 10:1 KJV After these things the Lord appointed other seventy also, and sent[21] them two and two before his face into every city and place, whither he himself would come.

Look Jesus sent out 70 more Apostles!

The word for sent here is *apostello* and not *apostolos.*

21

G649
ἀποστέλλω
apostello
ap-os-tel'-lo
From G575 and G4724; set apart, that is, (by implication) to send out (properly on a mission) literally or figuratively: - put in, send (away, forth, out), set [at liberty].

Even though the root is the same word the meaning is not as strong. *Apostello* simply means to be sent out or commissioned, these were disciples not apostles. Going back to a business analogy, it would be the equivalent to the top salesmen or supervisors, as opposed to management. They work to the policies already set and if they are not sure they go to the manager to be instructed in the proper protocol for a situation. Again I refer back to the traditional Jewish practice of sending out Shli'ach from the synagogue to carry out the business of the synagogue further afield.

Secondly Prophets. The inspired teachers – those that expound scripture.

Then teachers; - They would learn from the Prophets and preach and teach God's Word. They would do this in Power *(Miracles - Dunamis).*

Then the gifts of healing, noting that these occur after those that preach and teach the Gospel message. Signs always follow the message they do not precede it.

Then the practical gifts: helps, governing the body and working with the various languages required to minister to the congregation.

Context from a Judaic point of view places a different importance on this controversial passage of Scripture.

As most of us are in fact gentile believers grafted in, it is important that we go back to the roots and basics of the faith. We should also take on board the admonitions of Paul as they were written to us, the gentiles. If the early gentile believers were getting in this state and they had the teachers with them to show and explain the way, is it not arrogance on our part to assume Paul was only talking to the early gentile believers without a distinction. The Scriptures were written for us today as well. How we behave over the years has not changed, so we must take these instructions on board to understand why we are going wrong and correct our understanding and behavior.

The Father is the same yesterday, today and forever as is His Word. We need to be chastised and get back to where we can be most effective.

Walking in the Spirit of God, understanding our Faith, sharing the Word in Truth by the Spirit, and stop making God in our image as the Corinthian gentiles were trying to do.

Laying on of Hands

What about the laying on of hands to pass on the anointing?

There are Scriptures that appear to say we can pass on the anointing by the laying on of hands, let's look at some of these now, in context.

Act 8:17 KJV Then laid they *their* hands on them, and they received the Holy Ghost.

It was traditional for the Jews, in conferring favors, to lay their hand on the person receiving that blessing. Whether it was the Father passing on the inheritance to his son or the sin of Israel being passed onto the sacrificial lamb. Jesus would do this also, as did the apostles. This was a tradition that flowed through the entire Old Testament. The laying on of hands was showing agreement and association with whatever your hands were laid upon. A blessing was always passed on by the laying on of hands. It also showed the agreement by the person allowing hands to be laid upon them.

Hands have always played an important role in Judaism and Scripture. Hands are the parts of our body that can make things happen. It is with our hands that we can perform works, make repairs, deliver a child or carry a weapon. Hands are the part of the body that perform the physical tasks our minds wish to perform.

The hands are also a physical way in which we show worship to God *(raise Holy hands)*, or agreement with His expectations of us. Noah agreed with God by physically, with his hands, building the ark. The hands are always an outward sign of our agreement with something. Whether it is to kill in a war or pray for the sick, hands are the outward act of a conscious decision.

There are 438 verses in Scripture relating to Hands in the KJV. 333 of those are in the Tenach and 105 in the Brit Chadashah. So it is important to realise the relevance in relation to our misunderstanding today.

Acts 8:14 KJV Now when the apostles which were at Jerusalem heard that Samaria had received the word of God, they sent unto them Peter and John:
Acts 8:15 KJV Who, when they were come down, prayed for them, that they might receive the Holy Ghost:
Acts 8:16 KJV (For as yet he was fallen upon none of them: only they were baptized in the name of the Lord Jesus.)
Acts 8:17 KJV Then laid they *their* hands on them, and they received the Holy Ghost.

Remember from our earlier study that the gentiles were not baptized until Caesarea in Acts 10:44. That is an event which took place after this time. The Samaritans had a form of Judaism.[22]

---

[22] **Samaritanism** is the religion practiced by the Samaritan people. Like Judaism, it claims to be descended from ancient Israelite religion. It is closely related to Judaism in that it accepts the Torah as its holy book, though there are differences in the version accepted. Samaritans consider Jewish thinkers after the Torah as having been led astray while they themselves stayed to the true religion. Their

They still had to be proselytized back into Judaism to be accepted. As they had a form of relationship with the Spirit they were not fulfilled in the Spirit as the Jewish believers were, so the apostles laid hands on them to pray for the filling of the Spirit.

This was not them imparting the Spirit, but God releasing it to them via the agreement of the Apostle's prayer. This would have been seen by the Jewish believers as the proselytizing of the Samaritans into the faith as had been done many times before. Only this time into a relationship with the Jewish Messiah Yeshua. Seeing them receive the Spirit in this way would not surprise them. The Samaritans were not totally classed as gentiles but as apostates. Also note that there is no mention here of tongues being imparted. To the Jewish believers the Samaritans were already Jewish, just apostate as were many of the orthodox Pharisees and Sadducees.

> Act 9:17 KJV And Ananias went his way, and entered into the house; and putting his hands on him said, Brother Saul, the Lord, *even* Jesus, that appeared unto thee in the way as thou camest, hath sent me, that thou mightest receive thy sight, and be filled with the Holy Ghost.

As with Acts 8, this is a Jew not a gentile that has been brought to salvation. So the same understanding applies. Paul was filled in the Spirit as were the Jews at Pentecost.

---

temple was at Mount Gerizim, not Jerusalem.

Acts 19:6 KJV And when Paul had laid *his* hands upon them, the Holy Ghost came on them; and they spake with tongues, and prophesied.

Acts 19 is after the gentiles were baptized so how do we explain this?

If we read Acts 19:6 in the context of the story we can see why it is different.

Acts 19:2 KJV He said unto them, have ye received the Holy Ghost since ye believed? And they said unto him, we have not so much as heard whether there be any Holy Ghost.
Acts 19:3 KJV And he said unto them, Unto what then were ye baptized? And they said, Unto John's baptism.
Acts 19:4 KJV Then said Paul, John verily baptized with the baptism of repentance, saying unto the people, that they should believe on him which should come after him, that is, on Christ Jesus.
Acts 19:5 KJV When they heard *this,* they were baptized in the name of the Lord Jesus.
Acts 19:6 KJV And when Paul had laid *his* hands upon them, the Holy Ghost came on them; and they spake with tongues, and prophesied.

Acts 19:2-5 explain quite clearly when realizing that the people spoken of were not believers but were truly seeking after the truth and understood the need for repentance. They were baptized into John but had no understanding of who Yeshua was; only that someone would follow John. Paul explained to them the full Gospel message and they then accepted Yeshua and were baptized in His name. After this he went into to the synagogue to preach to the Jews.

It is the Holy Spirit that baptized them and filled them. Paul laying on his hands was a customary gesture, and not how the Spirit was imparted. We have already established that the Spirit is given by God at the time of salvation, if not we could not be saved and maintain our position of salvation in the first place. (The Spirit is given to help us obey and keep Torah)

If Paul could in fact give the Spirit as and when he chose, this would take away the Holiness of the Spirit and make it something sinful man could control. We know this is not possible as the Father, Son and Holy Spirit are one and sin cannot be in the presence of God, nor would God allow His Spirit to be commanded by the sinful nature of man. God is Holy.

The laying on of hands - was an act of "prayer," expressing an invocation to God that he would impart the blessing to "them." There was no anointing being passed on. It was a customary gesture when a "favor" was to be conferred or a blessing imparted.

If only a good anointing was passed on with the laying on of hands, Israel could not have passed on its sin to the sacrificial lamb.

Numbers 8:9 KJV And thou shalt bring the

Levites before the tabernacle of the congregation: and thou shalt gather the whole assembly of the children of Israel together:

Numbers 8:10 KJV And thou shalt bring the Levites before the LORD: and the children of Israel shall put their hands upon the Levites:

Numbers 8:11 KJV And Aaron shall offer the Levites before the LORD *for* an offering of the children of Israel, that they may execute the service of the LORD.

Numbers 8:12 KJV And the Levites shall lay their hands upon the heads of the bullocks: and thou shalt offer the one *for* a sin offering, and the other *for* a burnt offering, unto the LORD, to make an atonement for the Levites.

Numbers 8:13 KJV And thou shalt set the Levites before Aaron, and before his sons, and offer them *for* an offering unto the LORD.

The laying on of hands is a symbolic act. It is God by His Spirit that does any work involved with the laying on of hands through prayer.

2 Timothy 1:6 KJV Wherefore I put thee in remembrance that thou stir up[23] the gift of

---

23

G329
ἀναζωπυρέω
anazōpureō
an-ad-zo-poor-eh'-o
From G303 and a compound of the base of G2226 and G4442; to *re-enkindle:* - stir up.

God, which is in thee by the putting on of my hands.

That thou stir up the gift of God (*Greek - that you "re-enkindle")*. The original word used here denotes the kindling of a fire, as by a bellows, etc.

The idea is that Timothy was to use all proper means to keep his passion for Christ burning within him, and more particularly his enthusiasm for the great cause to which he had been set apart. However rich the gifts which God has bestowed upon us, they do not grow of their own accord, but need to be cultivated by us. We need to grow and continue in the faith. Not let it slip away with our focus going back to the world. We should not be distracted.

The language used here, "by the putting on of my hands," is just what Paul, or any other one of the elders or leaders, would use in referring to the ordination of Timothy.

It is like the way an older Presbyterian, Congregational or Baptist minister would address a pastor whom he had ordained. Nothing would be more natural than to remind him that his own hands had been laid on him when he was set apart for the work of the ministry.

Paul specifies in the next verse 2 Timothy 1:7. It is "the spirit of power, and of love, and of a sound mind." The meaning is that these had been conferred by God, and that the gift had been recognized by his ordination. It does not imply that any mysterious influence had gone from the hands of the 'ordainers', imparting any holiness to Timothy that he had not already received by the

Spirit.

> 1 Timothy 5:22 KJV Lay hands suddenly on no man, neither be partaker of other men's sins: keep thyself pure.

This Scripture is often quoted by the proponents of the faith movement and those that believe the anointing is passed on by us to others. They claim it means 'be careful who you give the Spirit to' as in Acts 18.

> Acts 8:18 KJV And when Simon saw that through laying on of the apostles' hands the Holy Ghost was given, he offered them money,

This is not the meaning of the Scripture in 1 Timothy. It is talking of ordaining people into the ministry. As opposed to Acts 8:18 which is demonstrating the Holy Spirit cannot be passed on willy nilly by selling it or giving it away oneself. Only Adonai can bestow the gift of the Spirit, only He decides who receives it.

> Numbers 27:20 KJV And thou shalt put *some* of thine honor upon him, that all the congregation of the children of Israel may be obedient.
> Numbers 27:21 KJV And he shall stand before Eleazar the priest, who shall ask *counsel* for him after the judgment of Urim before the LORD: at his word shall they go out, and at

his word they shall come in, *both* he, and all the children of Israel with him, even all the congregation.

Numbers 27:22 KJV And Moses did as the LORD commanded him: and he took Joshua, and set him before Eleazar the priest, and before all the congregation:

Numbers 27:23 KJV And he laid his hands upon him, and gave him a charge, as the LORD commanded by the hand of Moses.

This was a historical Judaic way of working in agreement with God. Nothing physical or spiritual was passed on. Only agreement was shown in respect to the ministry of Joshua.

Do not be in a hurry to ordain someone into the ministry who is not fit to be there (false teachers for instance). We are not to partake of their sin or teachings. Stand right before the Lord.

1 & 2 Timothy are explaining what type of person should be brought into the ministry. In fact 2 Timothy 2:15 states in no uncertain terms what a teacher should be doing.

Study to shew thyself approved unto God, a workman that needeth not to be ashamed, <u>rightly dividing the word of truth</u>. KJV

In today's church circles the laying on of hands has become something other than an outward sign of agreement, it has become a way of passing on the anointing from the anointed teacher or person. It has become a way that the "spirit" is passed from one person to another. The question is: what spirit is being passed on if it something we can do at will. Only God can change someone's heart and enable them to see the truth by His Spirit. So how would he give us the right to make that judgment on His behalf?

A comparison can be drawn between today's teachers and the Hindu Sidhus. Hindu teachers pass on the "anointing" through a system called shaktipat[24]. The shaktipat has long been practiced in such areas as yoga. Yoga is a Hindu way of worshiping their gods. Each exercise or movement is a worship position. All the Hindu statues and icons are striking these poses as they are claimed to be holy.

With yoga now so prominent in the west, and, for the most part becoming accepted by the mainstream believers as ok. Is it surprising that we see these occultic techniques being practiced and called Christian?

The laying on of hands has gone from: Glorifying God by showing we agree with Him in His promises and Blessings – to – We have the power to pass on because man is great as God has given us the power. The new teachings say that we are the children of God therefore we also have the power of God because we have been adopted into His family.

---

[24] **Shaktipat** is a <u>Sanskrit</u> word that refers to the act of a <u>guru</u> or <u>spiritual</u> teacher conferring a form of spiritual "power" or awakening on a disciple/student. "Shakti" translates as *energy* and "pat" as *touch*. Shaktipat can be carried out by the spiritually enlightened master either by transmission of sacred word or mantra, a look, a thought or by touch. The touch is usually given to the <u>ajna chakra</u> (Eyebrow Area) or <u>third eye</u> (Forehead) of the disciple.

God never promised us power for ourselves, but through the Holy Spirit to glorify the Father. As soon as we change the focus from God to man, we are accepting Satan's lie in the Garden of Eden: "You can be like the Most High"

Bibliography

1: Matthew Henry, ,

ABOUT THE AUTHOR

Though born in England, the author was brought up in Brooklyn NY within the Jewish community as his step-father was Jewish. After moving back to the UK at the age of thirteen his interests became more esoteric as he grew until eventually he became a Satanist. At the age of twenty-five he was miraculously saved by the Messiah Yeshua (Jesus) and as a result took to heart the scripture he was given at the time: 2 Timothy 2:15, Study to show yourself approved, a workman rightly interpreting the word of truth. After going to an Elim Bible College he spent years in ministries, for the most part reaching out to the Jewish people. CMJ – Churches Mission to the Jewish People, MT-Messianic Testimony, Emmaus Roadshow and recently through his own website and online ministry MDDL Discernment and Study Ministry - www.maxddl.org

He has now completed his Bachelors and Masters Degrees and a Doctor of Arts in Judaic Studies and is pursuing a PhD.

Other Books

- Biblical Interpretation Issues in Regard to the Torah or Law
- Rabbi Sha'ul – A Jewish Testimony
- A Question of Interpretation and Understanding
  - Feasts, Holy Days and Kosher, Are They For Today?
- How Did Paul Define The Gospel To The gentiles Without a New Testament?
- Christian Choices Today
- My Sheep Sleep

Also visit: Torah in Small Bites – A Video series examining Biblical topics from a Judaic perspective in an average of 13-15 minutes on YouTube.